CHEER
SKILLS
AND DRILLS

BY MARCIA AMIDON LUSTED

CONTENT CONSULTANT

Pauline Zernott
Spirit Director and Coach
Louisiana State University

SportsZone
An Imprint of Abdo Publishing | abdopublishing.com

ABDOPUBLISHING.COM

Published by Abdo Publishing, a division of ABDO, PO Box 398166, Minneapolis, Minnesota 55439. Copyright © 2016 by Abdo Consulting Group, Inc. International copyrights reserved in all countries. No part of this book may be reproduced in any form without written permission from the publisher. SportsZone™ is a trademark and logo of Abdo Publishing.

Printed in the United States of America, North Mankato, Minnesota
082015
012016

THIS BOOK CONTAINS
RECYCLED MATERIALS

Cover Photo: Shutterstock Images
Interior Photos: Christopher Futcher/iStockphoto, 4–5; iStockphoto, 6, 7, 10–11, 12, 14–15, 22–23; Jacom Stephens/iStockphoto, 6–7; Christopher Badzioch/iStockphoto, 9; Mike Powell/Digital Vision/Thinkstock, 13; Aleksei Lazukov/Shutterstock Images, 16–17; Andrew Rich/iStockphoto, 18; Shutterstock Images, 20, 24, 25, 28; Aaron Hernandez/iStockphoto, 26–27

Editor: Mirella Miller
Series Designer: Maggie Villaume

Library of Congress Control Number: 2015945767

Cataloging-in-Publication Data

Lusted, Marcia Amidon.
 Cheer skills and drills / Marcia Amidon Lusted.
  p. cm. -- (Cheerleading)
 ISBN 978-1-62403-982-9 (lib. bdg.)
 Includes bibliographical references and index.
 1. Cheerleading--Juvenile literature.   I. Title.
 791.6/4--dc23

2015945767

CONTENTS

ONE

MOVING AND MOTION

Football players move across a bright green field. As the crowd roars at a touchdown, the cheerleaders jump up and down, waving their pom-poms and chanting. At halftime, they perform a cheer, which may include stunts or a pyramid.

Cheerleading is fun. Some people also consider it a sport. It takes strength and training to be a good cheerleader. Most cheerleaders begin in middle school or high school. But you can learn basic cheer skills any time!

Cheerleading is a fun and high-energy activity.

ARM MOVEMENTS

One arm out straight and the other bent is the bow and arrow.

Motions are used to attract the attention of the crowd. Motions should be sharp and tight. All of these motions are easy to learn.

Arms stretched out with the elbows bent in is the half-*T* shape.

Arms are held in a high or low V position, raised in the air, or down by the sides.

LEG MOVEMENTS

Basic leg movements are important. The most basic is standing with the feet apart. Raising one knee and balancing on the other leg is called a hitch. Standing with one foot digging into the ground and the other leg straight is called a dig. There are also lunges, with one leg forward and the other back or out to the side.

Arm and leg movements are combined to make motions. Motions can be put together with words to create a sideline or chant, such as "Let's Go, Tigers!" There are special steps forward and backward called a pivot. It is also fun to create these moves. After the basics, it is time to learn more challenging cheer moves.

Combining basic movements makes routines more challenging.

TWO

JUMPS AND TUMBLING

Jumps are the next important cheerleading skill to learn. Jumps can be easy, such as jumping straight up. Or they can be difficult, like doing a toe touch and touching the toes in midair.

Every jump has the same three parts, no matter how hard it is. The first part is the approach and lift, also called the prep. This means setting up the jump and getting the body into a lifted position. The jump body position is the actual jump. Just as important is the landing, where the body comes back down to the ground. Landing properly with feet together and knees slightly bent prevents injuries.

Adding jumps makes cheerleading routines more interesting.

Most cheerleading moves require a lot of strength and flexibility.

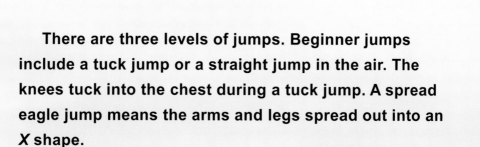

The C jump is a fun jump to try.

There are three levels of jumps. Beginner jumps include a tuck jump or a straight jump in the air. The knees tuck into the chest during a tuck jump. A spread eagle jump means the arms and legs spread out into an *X* shape.

Intermediate jumps include the herkey, where one leg is straight and the other is bent behind. The side hurdler is another jump with one leg straight and the other bent to the side. A more difficult intermediate jump is a pike. A cheerleader jumps into the air and folds in half, touching fingers to toes. Then he or she lands with slightly bent knees.

THE HARDEST JUMP

The hardest cheerleading jump is called Around the World. It starts out as a pike jump, then in midair, the legs are snapped open to a toe touch.

Advanced jumps are the hardest. There is the toe touch, where the legs are apart in a straddle split and the cheerleader touches their toes. The front hurdler jump has one leg forward and the other leg back. The body folds in half with the hands touching the toes in the pike jump. These jumps take a lot of practice. You can do stretches to train your body for jumps.

Once a cheerleader learns all of these jumps, he or she can combine them with other movements and add them to a routine. And to make the routine even more exciting, the next set of skills to learn is stunts!

The front hurdler jump requires a lot of practice and training.

14

THREE

STUNTS
AND SPOTTERS

In cheerleading, stunts are lifts usually done with several people. Stunts might include creating a pyramid or tossing a cheerleader into the air. Stunts are amazing to watch, but they can also be very dangerous. It is easy to get hurt if the stunts are not done properly. Stunts require training, a good coach, lots of practice, and spotters. Spotters watch the cheerleaders doing the stunt, look out for hazards, and are ready to catch the cheerleaders if they fall.

The spotter, *left*, must watch the cheerleaders during stunt practices too.

There are three different levels of stunts. One of the simplest beginner stunts is the pony mount. One cheerleader climbs on the back of another, arms placed in the air. The cheerleader at the top of the stunt is a "flyer." This means you are at the top of the stunt. The base cheerleaders hold the flyer in the air. There is also the double base thigh stand. Two cheerleaders stand side by side with their inside legs close, knees bent, and feet in front of each other. Their outside legs are spread out for support. The flyer stands with one foot on each base person. Then the base cheerleaders hold the flyer's feet in place.

Intermediate stunts include the elevator. Three base cheerleaders raise and hold the flyer up by the feet. In the scorpion stunt, the flyer stands on one leg, while stretching the other leg behind her head and grabbing her foot.

The base cheerleaders must hold the flyer so she does not fall.

With more practice, teams can work on harder stunts.

Advanced stunts, such as the toss to hands, require a lot of practice. The base cheerleader tosses the flyer into the air and grabs her feet, holding her up while the flyer does a high *V* with her arms. Then the flyer is tossed back up and caught as she comes back down. Pyramids and other balancing stunts are also advanced stunts.

It is easy for cheerleaders to get hurt trying stunts they are not ready to do. They must have proper equipment, plenty of spotters, and a place to perform without holes, rocks, or other hazards.

TIPS FOR SPOTTERS

Spotters have the most important job on a cheerleading team. They must always watch their flyer and use hands-on spotting. They must listen for their flyer to say "down," and they must never get distracted. The flyer's safety depends on them. The spotter assists with the stunt using hands-on spotting until it is mastered. Once the skill is mastered, the spotter stands next to the stunt, ready to catch the flyer.

FOUR

FUN
FORMATIONS

Cheerleading routines include many formations and transitions. Many cheerleaders do formations together. Formations are named for when team members stand in a specific pattern. Formations become fun and exciting when they are combined with other moves and stunts, while cheerleaders move around the field or the gym from one formation to another.

The simplest formation is bowling pins. Team members stand in a triangle similar to how bowling pins are set up. Windows, or staggered line formations, have team members standing in two lines, staggered. Formations also include cheerleaders standing as partners or arranged in diagonal lines.

Standing in windows means each cheerleader can be seen while in formation.

It is fun to see what stunts a team performs.

Formations would be boring if cheer teams simply stood still. A typical routine has the team starting in a formation such as bowling pins, transitioning through other formations, and adding jumps or stunts. Three flyers might be tossed into the air in a toss to hands stunt. Several team members might rise above the group in an elevator stunt. Or the entire team might finish in a pyramid. The creative part of cheerleading is how different cheer skills are combined to create a fun routine that entertains the crowd and gets everyone excited.

Elevators are common stunts that many cheerleaders on a team can perform together.

FIVE

STAYING ON TOP

Cheerleading is more than learning the basic movements and positions. Cheerleaders are athletes. They must train constantly and practice their skills. They need to exercise and build their strength. Cheerleaders must also stretch before they train or perform to avoid injury. They should wear proper clothing, always warm up before practicing or performing, and use a spotter for stunts. Cheerleaders should never try any skill or stunt that is too difficult for them. They need to eat well, drink plenty of water, get enough sleep, and be as fit as possible.

It is important to be prepared for each practice in order to learn more skills.

Cheerleaders are also members of a team. This means trusting and learning to work well with teammates. This is especially important between flyers, bases, and spotters. Teams also need to be creative together. Even with a coach to help create routines, cheer teams should work on their own ideas for formations and movements.

These are the basics. Motions, jumps, stunts, and formations, along with teamwork, create a solid foundation for becoming a great cheerleader!

ALL SHAPES AND SIZES

Cheerleaders on television and in movies come in every shape and size. Cheerleaders who are flyers have to be tossed in the air or climb to the top of a pyramid. People with smaller body types are good flyers. Flyers need stronger cheerleaders to act as their base. Base cheerleaders must be able to throw, catch, and support the flyers. It is important for all cheerleaders to be fit and athletic.

Being part of a cheer team can be a lot of fun!

GLOSSARY

ATHLETE
Someone who is good at sports and other kinds of exercise.

COACH
The person responsible for managing and training a sports team.

FLYER
The member of a cheer team who is tossed into the air during a stunt.

FORMATION
An arrangement or pattern that cheerleaders stand in during a routine.

HAZARD
A danger or risk.

INJURY
A wound, cut, or other kind of hurt to the body.

PIVOT
To turn or spin in one specific place.

SPLIT
Leaping in the air or sitting with legs straight out to each side.

SPOTTER
A person who watches or helps a cheerleader to keep him or her from getting hurt.

STUNT
An exciting and sometimes dangerous move or jump during a cheer routine.

FOR MORE INFORMATION

BOOKS

Gassman, Julie. *Cheerleading Really Is a Sport*. Mankato, MN: Stone Arch Books, 2011.

Lusted, Marcia Amidon. *Spirit-Raising Cheers and Chants*. Minneapolis: Abdo, 2015.

Webber, Rebecca. *Varsity's Ultimate Guide to Cheerleading*. New York: Little, 2014.

WEBSITES

To learn more about Cheerleading, visit **booklinks.abdopublishing.com**. These links are routinely monitored and updated to provide the most current information available.

INDEX

ABOUT THE AUTHOR

Marcia Amidon Lusted has written more than 100 books and
500 magazine articles for young readers on many different subjects from
animals to countries to rock groups. She is also an editor and a musician.
She lives in New England.